# Invitation to Believe

# Acclaim for
## *Invitation to Believe*

"Julie Schelling's book, *Invitation to Believe* offers everyone a guide book on your journey through life. It can help you to find faith and understand why. We are all divine creations and with Julie's guidance you can find your inner divinity. I love the word guidance: God, you and I, dance. We are all one family and children of God. There is a unity related to where we have all come from and as a surgeon I can add: we are all one family, the same color inside. With her help you can find faith, the true God of creation and stop fearing separation from your Lord. You will learn how to become complete, authentic and to choose life. Your afflictions will become your teachers and labor pains of self-birth which will help you to heal and become God with skin on. She talks about understanding and I can tell you that God wants you to understand why. We don't have a perfect world because a perfect world is not creation it is a magic trick. Life is a school and we are all here to live and learn so start your education by reading this book."

**Bernie Siegel, MD**, author of
*The Art of Healing* and *A Book of Miracles*

# Invitation to Believe

## Establishing Faith in the
## Universal Power

*Angie,*
*Wishing you*
*much peace*
*and love!*

*Best,*
*Julie*

## Julie R. Schelling

Coaching for Resonance
P.O. Box 963
Narberth, PA 19072
www.invitationtobelieve.com

Library of Congress Control Number: 2013957594

Schelling, Julie R..
Invitation to Believe / Julie R. Schelling.
Narberth, PA: Coaching for Resonance, 2014
p. cm.
Trade paperback: 9780990592006
Also available in Kindle and Epub versions.
1. God.  2. Universal Power.  3. Faith 4. Self-Help 5. Self-Development 6. Personal Growth 7. Meditation 8. Religion & Spirituality 9. Spirituality 10. New Age 11. Sufism 12. Enlightenment I. Title.

Cover illustration: Michael Green
Graphic design: Lawrence Didona
Back cover photograph of Julie Schelling: Angela Wahlgren
Editors:
William J. Connelly
Myra Diaz
Ameena M. Schelling

Printed in the United States of America
First Printing

With deep gratitude and appreciation to William J. Connelly, Myra Diaz, Ameena M. Schelling, Ahsiya Posner Mencin, Nurul Karimah Maschwitz, Dale Ann Applebaum, Donna M. Kaminski, Lawrence Didona, Michael Green, Malik Freudberg, Brenda Chase, David S. Tabby, DO, Martha Bardsley, MD, and Nathalie S. May.

# Contents

In the Beginning     1

Life without Faith     33

Negative Energy     36

Pure Light is Positive Energy     37

Religion and Beyond     41

What is Faith?     45

STEP 1: How to Establish Faith     49

STEP 2: How to Clear the Land     53

STEP 3: Everything in Life is Perfect     57

STEP 4: Life is a Gift     61

STEP 5: Exist within Every Breath     65

STEP 6: Breathe     69

Last Word     71

About the Author     73

It is my hope to help others establish faith in the One Light that exists within. There is one Power of Pure Light that belongs to us all. I pray that this book brings comfort to those who have lost hope. May those who suffer in this world from the illnesses of the mind and body be rescued from the greatest bondage, self-doubt. May we each accept the invitation to discover the exaltedness of our birthright and to understand that the key to true liberation resides within our very own hands and heart.

# In the Beginning

---

I can remember sitting on the curb outside my house at age seven and looking up at the vastness of the sky, wondering, "If God created the world and everything in it, then who created God?" I asked my mother this question many times, but she could never answer it. Little did I know that this was the beginning of my spiritual journey, my search to find the Truth within the inner meanings of life.

As a small child growing up in the 1960s and '70s, I used to watch the Hallmark biblical movie specials, which I absolutely loved. They awakened something in me. I wasn't sure what it was, other than that I loved to hear stories about the prophets and God. As a young teen I began to outwardly search for God. I am of Jewish heritage and was brought up in a reformed congregation. Although I appreciated the religion, I did not find the spiritual satisfaction or fulfillment that my heart was yearning for. When I was fourteen I became a born-again Christian, but my interest soon faded, and I became a Messianic Jew. Although this path combined my Jewish heritage with my love for the prophet Jesus, after a few weeks I again began to feel that it just didn't fit. I knew that the Universal Truth I was seeking would resonate within my heart as soon as it was found.

I often compared my spiritual quest to P. D. Eastman's children's book, *Are You My Mother?* In the book, a little bird hatches while his mother is gone, and he leaves the nest to go look for her. Since he is young and innocent, he asks the same question of everything he approaches: "Are you my mother?" I had the same naive openness in my quest. The little bird asked his questions without any understanding of what he was looking for, approaching everything with a childlike openness in his search for his true mother. I too was eager to adopt any belief I found, because I sincerely believed that the Truth existed. I also knew in my heart that if I kept looking, I would eventually find it.

Soon after starting a new high school, I noticed

a little stone church right next door to the building. One day I just walked into the chapel and sat down. It was completely empty, but the warm feeling I felt was overwhelmingly good. For some reason I could hear my prayers in a different way; they seemed somewhat louder, and for the first time I felt like something was listening to me. I felt a strong spiritual presence and love. Excited about my find, I decided to share the news with my closest friend. After hearing about my experience, she was eager to visit the church too. The next day we both went to the church and had similar experiences, so we agreed to meet at the church after school each day to pray. The chapel was always empty, so sometimes we would speak our prayers out loud like little children. I was grateful to have a friend who shared the same spiritual quest as myself, someone I could talk to about anything.

Even though I was now praying openly, I still did not feel that I knew much about God or where He existed. I wanted to know who God was and how to gain access to Him. I also wanted to understand how to converse with Him directly.

In 1976, at the age of sixteen, a classmate of mine gave me a book by M.R. Bawa Muhaiyaddeen, a revered holy man from the island of Sri Lanka in South Asia. The book was called *Songs of God's Grace*. The songs were filled with many wonderful passages of love and praise describing the beauty of God. From the moment I saw Bawa's picture on the front of the book and read a small verse on the back, I knew that I had found what I was looking for. My heart trembled as an inner recognition unfolded. A clear bell of Truth resonated within my heart as the outcome of this encounter. I knew without any doubt that I had to study with this enlightened teacher.

Bawa had established a Fellowship in the Overbrook section of Philadelphia in the early 1970s, which was only a short distance from where I was living. The classmate who had given me the book told me that Bawa was currently residing in Sri Lanka and would not be back in Philadelphia for another two years, so I attended weekly meetings at the Fellowship, where recorded discourses of Bawa were played. In one of the first talks I listened to, I heard something that truly made an impression on me. Bawa spoke about a primal state of spirituality that exists far beyond religion. This idea was something I could really identify with, since my own journey had led me to visit so many religions, even while understanding in my heart that God exists beyond any form and cannot be confined to any one teaching. I felt that Truth existed within everything, but I knew I was not mature enough to fully understand what this meant.

Bawa returned to Philadelphia in 1978, and I was anxious to finally meet him in person. Upon meeting him I was struck by the radiance of his face and the strength of his presence. His form was ever so slight, perhaps one hundred pounds or less. He clearly was old, but he didn't have any wrinkles. There was an aura of purity and grace about him. His face beamed with so much love and acceptance that I could not stop looking at him.

The minute he looked at me I felt like he was looking into my soul. Nothing in my life's experiences could compare to the profound feeling of that moment. If I had to describe it, it was partly a primal recognition and partly a feeling of coming home. I also felt a tremendous amount of fatherly love exuding from him—not the kind of love that a biological father might show, but a love that transcends the limits of blood attachments and partiality. Bawa's love was a love of divine justice, a love that showed no differences of "you" and "I", a love worthy of complete trust. For the first time in my life, I didn't need to look for the Truth. Bawa knew where it was, and if I studied with him, he would lead me to the source directly.

I had yearned to know God, and Bawa was the first person who could provide the explanations that made sense to me, not only on an intellectual level but deep within my heart, the very place from where my spiritual questions first arose. Bawa described God's manifestation as 3,000 beautiful qualities. He said it was our birthright as human beings to imbibe those qualities. We should treat all lives as we wish to be treated, and love all lives as one life. Upon hearing Bawa's words my heart melted in complete gratitude.

As I watched Bawa interact with everyone, I was beginning to see how he was able to lift up the hearts of those around him through his selfless love. I personally experienced this love when I met Bawa. Ever since I was a small child, I had felt like I was not as good as other people; I simply felt less important than others. I rarely felt special, and when I did, I was more preoccupied with losing that feeling than enjoying the moment. The very first time Bawa looked into my eyes, I immediately experienced his pure love for my soul. I felt I was truly valuable and special. With one look, he showed me the expansive precious gem that resided within my inner heart. It was as though his hand had gone deep inside my heart and pulled out a gem from a secret treasury, just to show me it was there. He exalted my life in that one moment. From that point on, my view of myself changed— not completely, but it marked the beginning of my journey inward to make a conscious effort to discover who I really was.

It was Bawa's divine selfless love that impressed me the most. He addressed everyone as "my precious jeweled light of my eye." Those were not mere words, I cannot fully express the rare magnitude of presence this humble man had. His actions and love for all people were clear evidence of his virtuous substance. The love that he exemplified came from a Power—a Power that, he taught, might be harnessed by anyone of sincere heart. Finally I had found the one guide whose love and wisdom could connect me directly to the source of the Truth I was seeking. A few years later, I traveled to Sri Lanka to study with Bawa.

With Bawa in Colombo, Sri Lanka 1982

For many, many years Bawa had lived in the jungles of Sri Lanka, meditating on God and studying the medicinal benefits of plants, shrubs, and trees. Wandering travelers from a variety of religions discovered Bawa, and he became well-known on the island for his unique wisdom and healing abilities. Soon after I arrived, I observed people from all over the island come to see Bawa. Each person would wait patiently for their chance to ask various things of him. Some would ask for prayers, others would ask for a medicinal remedy for a sick family member. Others came for money or food. Some simply wanted to meet the wise sage who had come to the city of Colombo. Whatever each one came in search of, Bawa lovingly and patiently listened to their needs and gave accordingly. Day after day I watched in awe as Bawa tended to the vast multitude of people who visited. I witnessed so many things—it was an extraordinary time for me.

As time went on, I knew that all I wanted to do was to spend as much time as I could with Bawa. I made a point to always be present for his discourses and to be available to help with any projects he would start. One of the things Bawa did was to cook huge amounts of food. He would use 20- or 40-gallon pots and often serve over one hundred or more people at a time. Along with others, I spent a lot of time cutting vegetables for the large quantities of food needed. Bawa would always add the spices himself, and he did so very carefully and precisely. He told us that if we used certain spices when cooking, we could prevent various illnesses and stay healthy. His curries were extremely spicy! I first learned to merely tolerate them, but within a short time I began to crave them. When the curries were ready, he would serve each person individually. As each one approached, he would look at their face, give a gentle nod of acknowledgment, and then serve them with intense concentration. Regardless of how many people were in line, he would do this until everyone was served. I had never tasted food like this before— it felt like divine medicine for my body.

I remained in Sri Lanka for one year.

After returning to the States, I continued to study with Bawa, who resided at the Philadelphia Fellowship, until his passing in 1986. During my ten years with him I felt I had to absorb as much information as I was able. Like a squirrel that stores away nuts for the winter, I wanted to gather everything. I knew that even though I did not understand everything, one day I would come to know. I knew that spending time with this rare sage, Bawa Muhaiyaddeen, was pure grace, and that the most important thing for me to do was to get as much of that grace as I possibly could. I knew that this mysterious treasury would sustain me throughout the days of my life.

Some referred to Bawa as a teacher, some as a guru, and others as a Sufi master. To me, he was a gentle, wise soul who treated me like his daughter. He taught me that there is One God, One Light, and One Life, and that we are all members of One Family. Bawa gave me many gifts, but the ultimate gifts were his words and living example of wisdom. He taught me that there is an inner guide that resides within the heart, which, if listened to, will always lead you to the Truth. Although Bawa passed away in 1986, the wisdom within his teachings continually guides me.

In 1998, my life took a difficult turn.

I was driving and approaching a red light when another car came speeding down the hill behind me and hit my left rear tire, which immediately blew apart. The other car continued side swiping the entire left side of my car. My eighteen-month old daughter was in the back seat. Thankfully, she was fine. I, on the other hand, was not. I felt a burning sensation down my neck, arm, and back. Little did I know that, over the next five years, I would suffer debilitating pain due to extensive nerve damage, or that I would travel to London for a specialized spinal fusion. My life changed completely in that one instant. I would never again be pain-free. Even as I write this, tears swell up in my eyes as I recall this challenging time in my life.

My children were ages eight, three, and one-

and-a-half, and it devastated me that I couldn't pick them up or play with them without hurting myself. All my dreams, all my ideas of how my life was supposed to be were now crushed. My previous reality had just died. I tried hard to control my thoughts, remembering Bawa's words of wisdom and constantly telling myself that it was God's will, that everything would be fine. I continued to tell myself: "Have faith, it will get better." It worked for a while, but as the years passed, my ability to fight my negative thoughts diminished. The doctors prescribed all kinds of pain medication that barely took away the pain. I tried every type of treatment: pills, cortisone shots, epidurals, acupuncture, a TENS unit, massage therapy, physical therapy, meditation, and even a morphine patch, which I wore for six months. Nothing seemed to work.

I was depressed, and felt like a discarded being. Witnessing my own state of mind was demoralizing. This path was so far removed from the life I had envisioned I would have on the "good path," the spiritual path. I convinced myself that my life had no purpose. All I wanted was for my pain to leave. Until then, I would never find happiness.

# Mind Song

*My heart is sore and breaking.*
*No one around.*
*The entire world is empty.*
*No one can see me or understand the depth of my*
*pain.*

*I see the good, but there is so much denied to me.*
*So many simple pleasures that I am to do without.*
*My heart is starving to be understood without words,*
*without explanation.*

*Will this end?*
*Can one endure such abuse?*
*My heart cries for comfort.*
*But none is to be found.*
*My heart fasts from being heard or seen.*

*Where is the end?*
*When will the spring come?*
*How much longer must I suffer in silence?*
*Will no help come?*
*Am I the only one who can help myself?*

*I am tired and weak, I want to sleep.*

*My tears flow, but there's no one to see.*
*My soul is imprisoned by an unjust world.*
*All I want is to be free.*

*Does one have to be imprisoned by one's past*
*mistakes?*
*By one's ignorance, by one's youth?*

*Unity. Peace. Kindness.*
*Compassion. Trust. Faith.*
*Love. Gentleness. Wisdom.*
*Can these not be obtained?*
*Will I die without this?*
*Is this forbidden to me?*

*Heavy is the heart that lies within me.*
*Tight is my chest as I feel the weight of my sadness.*
*Will I be rescued soon?*

*Will I?*

I have a vivid memory of one particular day. After having suffered years of pain, I was lying in my bed feeling emotionally numb, too depressed to get up. I was looking out the window, thinking about how much pain one person could suffer. Then, slowly, I felt myself letting go—of everything. I convinced myself that my life had no purpose. My entire existence was suffering in pain. I couldn't do anything for myself, my children, or anyone else. I didn't care anymore. It was easy to let go of this world and the pain in it. The world was rejecting me, there was nothing left for me. I was being squeezed out. As I watched my life pass in front of me, tears fell from my eyes. I let go.

I felt parts of the person I thought I was slowly dying inside—a cocky, opinionated, self-righteous person who thought she knew everything. The image of that person started to drift away. I began to view myself as someone who had been completely humbled, whose slate had been wiped clean. I was beginning to see things in a different way.

I realized how little control I had over what I wanted, and I surrendered myself to my circumstance. When one accepts life as it is, something profound happens. One finds peace. A silent knowledge emerged, reassuring my heart that everything was okay. Feelings of trust settled into my chest, the dawning of an inner strength.

Something wondrous was happening. I noticed a quieting of my usual thoughts and sensed a new presence residing within me. This presence felt like a trusted friend. As I contemplated it, my awareness began to observe a new inner dialogue. First a question from deep within my heart would rise up. As soon as it was heard, an answer would float effortlessly into view. The questions were profound. Questions like: If who we think we are, is more than just our bodies, then who else are we? The answers were just as impressive. Answers like: *We are a soul, a ray of God, which is one with God.* One by one, questions rose up, each question followed by an answer. What else exists within us? *Many things exist within us, truth and falsehood. The soul represents the true exalted potential of man. The ego, or false self, represents all things related to self-entitlement and concern for one's wellbeing.* Who stays and who leaves? *The answer of who stays or who goes depends upon which identity is chosen, the soul or the false identity.* Could this silent presence be the soul? *From the time we come in to this world, until the time we leave, the soul is silently present within.* Could the one who witnesses and the one who can bear anything be the soul? *The soul is not a product of this world, so attachments and suffering do not affect the soul. The soul is pure and one with God.* Could the pain in my body be reflective of the pain of a false identity? *Even if the smallest intention to know God is within the heart, God will do whatever He must do to uncover and reveal the true self, even if it can only be achieved through suffering.* Does the soul yearn to be known? *If the intention to know God is there, then the soul will yearn to be known. It is only in consciousness that the soul can connect man to God.* Could this suffering have acted as a gateway to liberation? *Through suffering, attachments to this world can be broken, opening the heart to truth and liberation. What first appears as bad sometimes offers the greatest gift.* Did I have to give up wanting everything before I could experience peace? *The inner heart must be cleared of worldly attachments before the treasure of peace can be given.* Perhaps as long as our ego is present, our soul cannot emerge? *The two cannot exist in the same place. Only the soul can be one with God, because the soul is a ray of light that comes from God Himself.* Maybe the false identity we have created is keeping us from knowing who we really are? *As long as we reside within the structure of the false identity, we will never understand who our true self is—the soul.*

Both the questions and the answers came with a clear, calm confidence that satisfied my heart with perfect precision. As I contemplated this interchange, I thought about how I had always wanted to know God. I wondered if this yearning had something to do with why I had undergone so much suffering in my life. In order for me to find God, He needed to remove whatever was blocking me from seeing Him—my false identity. Because I was resisting and not accepting what was occurring, I could not move forward spiritually. I would never wish the suffering that I experienced on anyone, but I do believe with all my heart that my car accident and all that followed was necessary for my spiritual growth.

Without the suffering I experienced, I would have never have let go of my previous identity; the grip of my mind would never have surrendered. And through experiencing immense suffering, I could now understand what others felt when they suffered deeply. I discovered a common connection, a unity, between myself, and others. It became one experience. It didn't matter what the causes or specifics of the suffering were, simply that it was identifiable as deep suffering. This unity of experience allowed me to connect with others in a profound new way, with authentic empathy and love.

True understanding comes from experience. My heart had been yearning for God as long as I could remember, and although I found teachings that had made sense to me, I really only understood a small portion of them. Learning from experience, however, gave new meaning to what I already understood intellectually. What did I learn? I learned that God loves us, and He will give us whatever it is that we want in our hearts. I wanted God, so He removed that which was blocking me from knowing Him. Thus, who I used to be was chased away so that my soul could be the conscious One in my life. Of course, I cannot say that my soul is the only one conscious all the time. My mind and ego are still players, but now I have a clearer understanding of their limitations and do my best to transcend them when needed.

I had believed that I had faith in God, but when I needed it the most, I was unable to utilize it. Faith is of no use if it cannot help you in your time of need. I thought I had faith, but I realized that I did not.

To me, faith is like fuel in an engine. Our soul is the vehicle, and our will is the driver. One can only drive the vehicle if one puts gas in the engine. The driver must pull up to the gas station, get out of the vehicle, and pump the gas. Only then will the vehicle be able to go where it needs to go. Similarly, if we are afflicted by certain difficulties and do nothing about it, we will only be able to go so far until our "gas" runs out. We have to do what it is in our own power to do: fuel our faith, and surrender the responsibility for whatever else happens, to God. Every time we surrender a thought of negativity to our faith in God, we are pumping more gas into our vehicle. Only then are we able to go where we need to go in our life.

I have learned that faith is effort-based, and that it requires my active participation. Faith is not just a thought, an idea, or a belief. Faith is complete trust in God. After this realization my life was restored little by little—not to where it had been before, but to a new state of being.

I have always held onto the belief that nothing happens without a reason.

After living with years of pain, in 2006 I was diagnosed with RSD, or Reflex Sympathetic Dystrophy. RSD is an autoimmune disease affecting the sympathetic nervous system, which causes a misfiring of nerve impulses. Although it manifests itself differently from patient to patient, the primary complaint of RSD is pain.

I was undergoing a two-week treatment session at a local hospital. A nurse guided me into a room with several other women. We were divided by curtains and hooked up to IVs and heart monitors. I could hear the other patients talking to the nurses, their voices heavy and depressed. They were complaining about the pain, each one sharing their specific location. Each one's complaints were different, but all of them were suffering. As I listened to them, I began to feel their heavy hearts, their sadness, their despair, and their utter hopelessness.

Although, I was suffering the same painful effects of RSD, I considered myself to be extremely fortunate. Over the many years that I lived with pain, I had come to the realization that I could make one of two choices—one was to be a victim of pain, and the other was to find a way out. Of course, when you have an illness and are suffering in pain, simply wishing it away is not sufficient. I realized that I didn't have control over my RSD, so I asked myself, what *do* I have control over? I have control over my thoughts and my beliefs. Okay, what about it? With respect to my beliefs, I believe that God is a Power who has ultimate control over all things. I also believe that nothing is random and everything happens for a significant reason. In addition, I believe I have faith in God, but utilizing that faith is something I needed to master in order to change my predicament. Since faith relied on trusting God, I had to fully understand what "trusting in God" really meant. I knew that just saying the mere words "I trust in God" wasn't enough. I needed to know what trust was. Trust, as defined by the dictionary*, is: *"reliance on the integrity, strength,*

---

* http://dictionary.com

*ability, surety, etc., of a person or thing: confidence.*"
Therefore, if that definition were applied to "trusting
in God," then for me to sincerely mean it, I would have
to let go of my preoccupation with the misfortune
of my illness and accept it as a reality ordained by
God. I would also have to be reliant on His integrity,
strength and ability and the surety that I was in good
hands. I don't have to especially like the situation—I
don't even have to understand it—but I do have to let
go of my frustration with it along with the baggage
of self-pity. If God is great and God wants this to
happen, then why fight it?

I realized that for me to have real faith, I
would have to utilize faith. So I decided to put
it into practice. I would slowly say, "I hand the
responsibility of this illness and this pain over
to you, God." Whenever my pain would come, I
would hand my burden over to Him by persistently
repeating that phrase. The result: the effects of my
pain would lessen. I began to change my attitude
by viewing my pain in a more practical sense.
Simply put, my pain and suffering just needed to be
managed. I observed that my RSD ran in cycles that
would begin soon after stressful periods. As the

onset of the RSD settled into a particular location, such as a small pain in my foot, I would observe it as it gradually intensified. As this occurred, I would declare, "Okay RSD, you do your thing, but no matter what you do, you will not control my thoughts or beliefs. You will not change my attitude or my trust in God, period!" So even though the RSD would attempt to settle in somewhere, there were many times when it would leave before getting really bad. I made it a point to push my awareness away from focusing on the pain and to actually pretend that it didn't exist. I noticed that in doing this, although the pain did not entirely leave, it would definitely decrease. I began talking to my RSD like a spoiled child that needed discipline.

Today, I won't give into it when it whines or nags me. I decide when I'll give it my attention, not the other way around. I believe that by addressing my RSD like it's a separate identity, this sends a clear message to my brain/RSD that there is new force to be reckoned with. It might cry like a baby, but when I tell it to stop, or that I don't care if it flares up, and I ignore it, it just gives up and retreats until the next time. I attribute the successful management of my

RSD to the ability to direct my thoughts in a positive direction.

The disease RSD may cause physical pain but it cannot affect my heart or my faith. The strength of my faith enables me to bear the pain with patience. I am by no means a martyr, so if I need to take pain medication when it gets really bad, I do. It is necessary to know how to manage the pain physically, mentally, and most importantly, spiritually. I may not have control over the disease itself, but I do have control over my will and my attitude. I made a firm commitment to myself that I was going to take back my life, and in doing so my suffering decreased.

As I was experiencing these realizations, the thought came to my heart: "I wish there was a way that I could share the faith and wisdom that I have found with those who have lost hope and faith in God. I wish there was a non-religious way to teach others how to tap into to the universal spirituality that lies within their own hearts. I wish there was a way to teach them what I have found." This was something I really wanted to do.

The next day, when my neurologist came to check on me, I brought up the idea of introducing spirituality to patients suffering from various illnesses or depression. I also suggested that it would be just as important to educate doctors on the subject as well, since they work so closely with their patients. My doctor, who is also an associate professor at a university hospital, thought this was a great idea and asked me to put something together. Motivated by his encouragement, I figured I would work on it a few days later, after my treatment had ended.

While undergoing one of my last treatments, I had a somewhat startling but enlightening experience. I felt myself leaving my conscious mind and being taken on a journey within myself. I felt like God was saying, "Come with me. I want to show you something." I found myself inside my physical body. I had no form, only awareness. My awareness was standing there inside my artery. Looking straight ahead, I saw blood flowing toward me, and then quickly branching out in another direction toward my heart. The inside of the artery was light pink, wet, and shiny, and there were tiny veins embedded in its wall. As I looked more closely at the rounded walls of tissue, I could see them quivering with a sort of energy or vibration. Wherever I looked, I could see the inner workings of my body. Each section was performing its function in rhythmic perfection. I felt tremendous harmony resonating within everything.

Next, I saw a cell come rolling toward me; it seemed huge and round. I effortlessly moved into it. It felt like entering inside an empty balloon. The inside felt extremely alive and was gently pulsating. It was empty at first, but soon afterward, I saw another cell rolling toward me. I then moved into this one, just as I had with the first cell. I would see nothing at first, and then another cell would appear. This process continued for a while. Even though I kept moving into each cell within a cell, none of them were touching each other; each one was sort of suspended in a formless realm. As I entered into each new cell, the previous one disappeared.

As this was happening, there was no sense of the self I knew prior to this experience, just an open awareness of what was being witnessed. It was understood that what I was witnessing was the Power of God, the Power of Life itself. Using my body as the example, I was being shown that the existence of God is intermingled within the smallest cell within the smallest cell. This was an exhilarating and profound realization. I already believed that God existed within and without all things, but I didn't understand it until this extraordinary moment.

Next, I saw my body as if it were lying down a few feet in front of me. Then, a glowing green form sat straight up at my waist section. I understood this form to be my light-body, or the soul that is one with God. As soon as that understanding came, the glowing form laid back down into my body.

I realized that there is not an atom in existence that can deny the presence of God. God is everywhere; His presence is intermingled within and without all things, both seen and unseen. At that very moment, I also realized my immateriality. I understood that the only thing that truly exists is God and God alone.

My previous identity—the "I", the one that I thought to be myself—was exposed as being artificial. I was shown the truth of life. As I became aware of this truth, I began to get scared. The thought of my old self and physical body seemed foreign and out of reach. I felt so far away and lost, like an astronaut who has been abandoned in outer space. I was now a visitor, visiting the one who had just witnessed the inner body journey. "Where do I go?" Thoughts of fear that I was going to die flooded in. I tried to bring myself to move my body or to speak, but I couldn't. The thought came, "Okay, this may be it; this may be what it's like when people say that they die or have out-of-body experiences and they can't get back." I waited a while—scared that I might not come back, or that if I did, I would never be the same, because my identity had now been altered. All that I had just experienced inside my body seemed to drift to the background. I was confused. Fear had taken over.

At that moment a nurse came in and, to my surprise, I managed to utter words: "I almost died." The nurse immediately hurried away to call the other nurses to come. I slowly came to. Shortly afterward, a friend arrived to pick me up, and as soon as I saw her I began to cry. I was not fully aware of what had just happened. I could barely speak to her, but managed to share a little. She lovingly listened.

I was shaken and somewhat in shock, so my friend helped me home and put me in bed. I became silent within myself. The idea of explaining to my family what had just occurred seemed pointless. At the time, I couldn't even assess it, let alone articulate it. It was an experience for me to understand, myself alone, so I just let it sit within my heart, waiting to see what was next.

The following day was my final day of treatment. After I returned home, as I lay in bed, I found myself eager to work on the spirituality book, so I opened my laptop and began to type. From the first word, I began to feel the same vibration and power that I had experienced the previous day during my inner body experience. I could not hold back the words. I had never experienced anything like this, had never before written anything longer than a letter. My heart felt like a fresh spring that had just been tapped and would not stop flowing. My heart was typing, and my body was shaking. The strangest thing throughout my writing process was that there was no input from my intellect or thoughts. Rather, the book just flowed out of my heart with great force. I typed for the next few days straight until it was finished.

I am not sure how to explain the mystery of this next section, as it is a true mystery to me. It is my sincere prayer that you will find some benefit by reading it. There is One Light and One Life, and we are all members of the One Family.

# Life without Faith

What does it mean to live a life without faith?

We all share the common experiences that comprise life in this world. When we are young we learn from our parents, we play, go to school, learn how to read and write, have friends, have relationships good and bad, go on to further our education, leave home, get a job, get married, have kids, get old, and eventually die. In our life we may experience good or bad health, wealth or poverty. Depending on these experiences we share similar feelings of joy, sadness, happiness, sorrow, elation, disappointment, acceptance, rejection, pride, humility, selflessness, selfishness, truthfulness, dishonesty, love, hate, comfort, hurt, hastiness and remorse. So many emotions are intermingled within each experience.

Our sense of self, our identity, is created by variations of genetics, personality, early upbringing, life experiences, and the uniqueness of the inner heart. The first four are perhaps easier to understand, but the inner heart is the real mystery.

When we are young, we are not adequately prepared for the life ahead. We are brought up to believe that what is "good" is what we want, and what is "bad" is what we don't want. These black and white definitions vary, but for the most part we share similar social views. When we enter young adulthood, we start to think about our future, wanting some of the same things. For example, we want a good education, a good job, a good spouse, a good house, good children, a lot of money, good health and, most significantly, to always be happy.

The problem begins when we are confronted with something we define as "bad", and we immediately become sad and flustered. When "bad" things happen, we often attribute them to having bad luck or misfortune. After suffering through several such negative occurrences we begin to think we have been singled out and ask "Why me?" internalizing these disappointments as personal assaults. We try to brush off the "whys" of these occurrences as purely random, but over time this becomes more difficult to do. Our ability to rationalize eventually weakens, leaving us emotionally exhausted and defeated.

As the days of our life pass, we accumulate more and more wounds, to the point where we bear no resemblance to our youthful selves. As we age, we continue to interpret these misfortunes as something bad that we deserve, causing our hearts to harden. This is a misconception, no matter how subtle it might be, that gets suppressed within our subconscious and leaves us with a deep-rooted sense of failure.

Over time, we become progressively sadder. Feelings of despair choke the meager remains of hope that exist, paralyzing the conscious mind and sealing its fate. The proud ego denies that this is true, but the inner heart admits its misery and cries for help.

This state is what I believe to be life without faith. Without self-reflection, one is powerless to make a positive change. Once we begin to understand the Universal Truth and our life's purpose as defined by the inner revelations that arise from within the inner heart, we can begin to emerge from the darkness of illusion and liberate ourselves from suffering.

# Negative Energy

Negative energy is a dark, poisonous force that wreaks havoc wherever it goes, destroying everything it touches. It gives rise to illness, sadness, hatred, and mistrust. When we don't understand this darkness, we become prey to every nightmare imaginable. Doubt is the father of negativity. We need to understand the nature of negativity and its purpose. Once we recognize its form, we may begin to utilize the tools of wisdom that can conquer its destructive powers.

# Pure Light is Positive Energy

Positive energy is a Pure Light. It signifies strong faith. It is melting love for one's true self and all of creation. It is a Power that cannot be compared or challenged. It is the Power of divine love, limitless compassion, and mercy. It is the gentle kindness of a baby. It is the purity of the inner heart. It is the true form of man. Without a shadow of separation, it is the oneness of being. It is complete understanding of the inner meanings. It is the resplendence of Truth. It is all of life. It is one. It is everywhere. There is no place it is not. It is within and without. It is without ego. It is the Power that creates, sustains, and nourishes. It is a father, it is a mother, and it is a baby. This Light, this Power, exists within and without all worlds—in the world we came from, in this world, and in the hereafter. The only thing that exists eternally is God's Pure Light.

This Power may be called by many names. It can be called God, Allah, Light, Muhammad, Moses, Jesus, Abraham, Buddha, Krishna, Positive Energy, Father, Love, Purity, and by many other names. I call it God, Light, or Father, but what is most important is the Power itself.

This Power can only be known through faith. This Power is available to all lives, not just a select few. It is the birthright of all humankind. This Power shows no separations of caste or color, of race or religion, whether one is rich or poor. This Light is undiminishing love. One can take and take from this Power and it will never be diminished. This Power is complete understanding. It is complete forgiveness.

This Power knows every soul, every thought, and every intention. You cannot hide from the light of this love. You need not fear this Power, for it is the One that gave life to life itself. There is nothing this Power cannot do. This Power is complete divine luminous wisdom. This Power resides within the inner heart of every human being. Every person can access this Power. This Power is the divine explanation of all things. This Power only wants you to succeed. This Power wants to draw you closer within It. This Power wants you to join with It. If we can understand Its greatness, trust in Its judgment, and then surrender to Its wisdom, then will we be able to merge with the Pure Light.

# Religion and Beyond

Many religions exist. There are many houses of faith, and most of us have some kind of tie to one religion or another. History has told its story in many different ways. Each religion came at a different time in the world in order to bring a particular teaching. Some of the witnesses of the prophets were the scribes who were responsible for recording the story of each religion. According to what has been written, the prophets and enlightened beings met with great suffering, and taught various lessons in accordance with their difficult experiences. To some degree, we are all descendants of these wise beings, bringers of truth, and bringers of peace. Whether or not these stories are true, they have remained in the world and have withstood the test of time.

These religions still exist in today's world,

welcoming believers to join them. Each religion is like a house with four walls, a roof, windows, and a floor, but how many may enter the door of each religion? Does one have to dress a certain way or think a certain way? Does one have to be a particular color or race? Can anyone join? Each religion has its own criteria for joining.

We, as human beings, know so little. We grow up in this world trying to learn as much as we can, compiling all of our studies and accomplishments. We boast of our religion and knowledge. We puff ourselves up with arrogance and self-pride. As we live our separate lives, we move further and further away from the Truth, trusting in only what our senses and intellect comprehend. We lose our ability to connect with others in unity. We distance ourselves from others so that we can avoid being affected by their happiness and sorrows. As we grow away from our true selves, we accumulate more and more false ideas. We convince ourselves that our beliefs are right and that others' beliefs are wrong. We leave no room for reflection and reasoning, furthering our isolation from one another. Instead of focusing on what unites us, we focus on that which separates us, making our hearts yet harder.

There is a house that has no walls, roof, windows, or floor. There is a house in which anyone can join. There is a house that is full of light. There is a house that can nurture each heart effortlessly. There is a house of unity, love, compassion, light, and kindness. This house is the house of Pure Light, Pure Positive Energy, and Pure Goodness. In this house, all are welcome. There are no stipulations for joining, other than simply walking in. This house holds the cure for illnesses of the mind, body, and soul. This house holds the key to liberation from the form. This house can remove the pain of the mind, pain of the body, and pain of ignorance. The door to this house is always open. This house exists beyond the suffering of this world. It is a refuge for all. This house brings lasting comfort to the soul. This house is the real home for every heart. This house is inner peace, inner silence, and inner contentment. This house is beyond religion. This house is the inner heart.

# What is Faith?

Faith is a belief in something you cannot see. If we were to say that we have faith in God's Pure Light, we would be able to rely upon that Power for everything in our life. Yet some confuse the notion of faith with believing in what is seen. That which we see is merely a physical fact. Thus, as long as everything is going smoothly in our lives, we think of ourselves as people of faith, but as soon as we perceive that something bad has happened, we fall completely apart.

Faith is a tool that needs to be understood. Faith is a tool, so only if it is utilized, is it beneficial. Because faith is based upon what is unseen, to say that one has faith is quite easy—but to truly have faith is another matter.

For example, let's say that you consider yourself to be a religious person who has faith, but then you are diagnosed with an illness. You may conclude that this affliction is an act of God's will. If this were to happen to you, would you be angry with God? Would you think this occurred because you are a bad person, or unlucky? For a person who has true faith, there would be trust that this act was not random and that, for some reason, some benefit could result of it. To have faith is to trust in the Power of God, to trust His judgment, to surrender all thoughts of doubt and resentment.

Developing an illness may be painful or even scary. No one can say that difficulties are not difficult. But the point to keep in mind is that everything happens for a significant reason. There may be something you need to see or realize that can only be achieved through this occurrence of an illness. Perhaps this illness has come to you for the purpose of directing your attention toward a deeper place inside yourself, toward your inner heart. We may not understand God's reasoning at first, but if we make a strong effort to patiently trust in His wisdom, then precisely at the right moment, the explanation will come. Often you don't even have to look for it; it will just be revealed to you.

In order for this explanation to come, one must be completely surrendered to God's judgment. One must hold the strong belief that His Pure Light contains divine justice. Even though we may not comprehend the "why" of His actions, if we can just be patient, striving to maintain faith, trust, surrender, and contentment, the inner meanings of Truth will emerge.

# STEP 1
# How to Establish Faith

If you have a plot of land, can you grow vegetables on it without first plowing the land? You must remove the rocks, sticks, and debris that lie upon the earth. This is the first step before you can plant anything. Every heart is like a plot of land. Each one is allotted the appropriate size and appropriate tools. Everyone is given the ability to grow his or her own crop.

The first step toward having faith is to believe, but how can you believe in something that you don't know? This is where you have to take a "leap of faith", let go of everything you have held onto before this point, and give it your best shot. It will be awkward at first, but you have nothing to lose. If your life is great now, and you are completely content, then you won't need to try this. This is for those who are searching for the truth of life, for those who are seeking the unconditional love that will never betray them. It is for those who want divine wisdom.

Next, select a name to call this divinely Pure Light, and then focus on it with complete earnestness. Make a declaration to that One Power that you will believe in It. Hold strong to this thought, no matter what the voices of your mind might try to say. It will require great effort at first, and you will have to put some trust in the unknown. But soon, less effort will be required, and the benefits it will bring to your life will be limitless. The proof of confirmation will come in due time, and it will not be in the form of miracles, but rather in a subtle, gentle new way of communication within the inner heart. You will need patience and perseverance to hold onto your newly established faith, but in time you will be shown the explanations contained within your inner heart, confirming that you are on the right track.

There was a time when I used to say that I had faith in God, yet when certain things occurred in my life, I fell apart. I went into a depression and felt lost. When the difficulties came, I did not know how to utilize the faith I thought I had, because I really didn't have any; I merely thought that I did. This was extremely difficult for me to accept, especially because I viewed—and admittedly, prided—myself on the fact that I was a person with strong faith. I suffered through that humbling realization for a long time. But later, something wonderful happened: real faith was born. My ignorance was dispelled, and room was made for the truth to come. Little by little, my newly introduced faith became a tool I could utilize in every way. For myself, it was only due to my difficulties that this grace was able to manifest and my newfound faith be born.

I can say with certainty that I believe in God, that Authentic Pure Power. God is a Light that has no darkness. He only wants His children to grow closer to Him, not farther away. I know that God doesn't want to harm me. I trust in Him completely. I know that God loves me because it is this Power that gave me my life. God is the One that gives me everything I have. God is the One that has given all lives what they have.

We have to firmly establish within our heart the intention that God exists. This is the first step in becoming aware of the plot of land in the inner heart.

# STEP 2

# How to Clear the Land

After you have declared your intention to the Pure Light of Grace, beseech His help. Implore Him, "Oh God, You are my Father, You are my Mother, You are my Creator. You know my inner heart. Forgive me for the faults I have committed, knowingly and unknowingly, protect me from hurting any lives, help me to reach You. Guide me and bestow Your divine wisdom so that I may understand my true self and, in turn, understand You. Please accept my plea. I humble myself at Your feet of infinite justice and melting love."

Whenever you are in need of guidance, recite this intention in your heart, and keep it alive by repeating it often.

Because this effort is new to you, doubts will flood your thoughts. The lawyer of the mind will make its case that what you are doing is a waste of time. It will explain why it is ridiculous, why nothing of any use will come of it. But you must let go of your old ways of thinking. Remember: You truly have nothing to lose by trying this. You can work at managing your thoughts by saying, "That's okay, I'm just going to try this," or, "Go away, you haven't helped me yet; I'm doing this now." Every time you can chase away a thought of negativity and replace it with a positive one, another karmic stick or rock is removed from your land. Each act that you accomplish by keeping true to your intention will be clearing away your past deeds and seeds of ignorance.

Little by little, you will have cleared the land. As you transcend the doubts, God will be able to plow your land. Whatever happens in your life, if you can surrender your negative thoughts and conclusions and hand them over to God, more and more work will be done on your land. If you do the work of maintaining faith in Him, He will do your work for you. This will take a lot of time, but the benefits will be unimaginable. Patience, contentment, and trust in God will then carry you through your life.

This journey is undertaken alone. To understand

this story of life is everyone's birthright.  If you can make your faith strong, nothing will be able to harm you. By dealing in this way with everything that comes to you, you will be able to let go of the negative weights and live in peace.

## STEP 3
# Everything in Life is Perfect

---

If we were God, we would know everything. We would know that there is an explanation for everything. Nothing is random. If we were God, we would understand the inner meanings of life itself. We would not worry about anything, because we would be in full control.

There is a delicate balance in nature. Are we not also a part of nature? Every creation experiences birth and death—trees, flowers, insects, animals, cells, atoms, illnesses, cures, the sun, the moon, the stars, the ocean. Does life need us to exist? When we die, does life in this world stop? If life can go on without us, why do we think we are so important?

Truth is what is important. Isn't that what we really want? Is there anything else that could be more valuable? If we truly understand the Pure Light, we will accept that everything is in accordance with His will.

We flatter ourselves, thinking how big we are, how brilliant our opinions are, but we really praise ourselves as a way of concealing our ignorance or insecurities or doubts. The inner heart knows the truth, but we are afraid to listen because we do not have faith. We do not know God's love and the immensity of His power. Yet He is intermingled within every life. If we can recognize this and give Him the proper respect, our lives will begin to improve.

We can make our faith grow by taking each difficulty and handing it over to God, giving all responsibility to Him, but this does not mean that we do not have to do our part. In every situation, we must do what we can do. Whether it is going to the doctor when we are sick or taking our medicine, we must do what we can. If we are hungry, God has given us the means to feed ourselves. If we do not feed ourselves we will die. Like that, we must not be lazy and think God will do that which we are responsible for doing. It is only after we have done our share that we may surrender the rest to the Pure Light. Allow

God to carry the weight as we do our duty; let Him do His duty. We must know our role and our duties and perform them with good qualities.

# Life is a Gift

If we were to truly understand God's Infinite Power, we would see that everything we see, hear, touch, smell, feel, and experience is a gift. If we could appreciate all that God has given us, we would be content at all times. If we could fully appreciate the gift of our life, we would understand the meaning of contentment. Therefore, from the time we take our first breath in this world until the time we take our last, we must strive to understand the purpose of our life. It is within the mystery of our very breath that we can communicate with the Giver of Life.

We experience so many things. Sometimes events make us sad, so we cry. When we feel happy, we may laugh, and that's all right. It is only when we magnify these experiences, along with their associated emotions, that we make ourselves crazy. Everything we experience is an opportunity for learning and should be examined very carefully. The true purpose of these experiences is for us to extract the point of wisdom within them. However, we inadvertently miss the point, becoming enamored with the drama and outward aspects. This pattern creates difficulties that cause sadness. Everything in our life is a gift for us to gain awareness. It is out of His love that God provides us with these lessons, so that we can better understand ourselves and, in turn, better understand Him.

We may be on this inner journey alone, but we are not alone in this world. We have one another. Because we do not understand our own lives, we do not understand the wealth that God has given to each one of us. There is a point of Light within every heart. When we can discover that point within our own heart, we will begin to see that same point of Light in others. We will understand that we are all brothers and sisters of the One Light, and that we are all a part of the same family of humankind.

Don't others experience happiness or suffering just as we do? If we were to receive a raise in pay at our job, would we not feel joyful about it? Likewise, wouldn't a co-worker feel the same joyful feeling if they were to receive a raise in their pay? If we break our arm and suffer pain, would not our brother feel the same pain if his arm were broken? It is to the exact extent that we understand ourselves that we are able to understand others.

If we can see our life as a gift, then we will feel appropriate gratitude for the One who has given us this life. Because we do not understand Truth, we find fault with God and with others for not giving us what we want. We live selfishly, wanting only to fulfill our own desires. When things don't go our way, we become sad and bitter, blaming everything and everyone. We must understand that to live a life of Truth, we have to divorce ourselves from the selfish chatter of our minds and listen only to the selfless truth within our inner hearts.

If we can learn to value our own inner heart, we will come to value the inner hearts of others. It is only by connecting with the love within our own hearts that we become capable of sharing that love with the love in the hearts of others. If we understand that we are all born from the One Heart Of Light and that everything is perfect, we will feel God's love and protection at all times.

If we can do what we came into this world to do—to understand whom we really are and to understand who God is—we will progress on our journey and reach the inner heart. Then we can share that wealth with every life that crosses our path. We have to keep our faith strong by continually surrendering our difficulties over to God. If we can do this, then that inner plot of land will become a bountiful crop that benefits all lives.

Gratitude is the key to contentment. Once we achieve this state, we will live a life of true peace, perceiving everyone as one family, one life. In this state alone, we will experience the fullness of perfection.

# STEP 5

# Exist within Every Breath

The essence of life is contained within every breath we take. The ultimate gift that God has given us exists within the mystery of the breath. Trust, faith, love, and gratitude are contained within the breath. If we can understand this subtlety and come to know the secrets that lie within it, we can reach true liberation from the sufferings of this world.

Without breath, there is no life. We need air to live, but without the ability to breathe, the air is of no use. The secret within the inner meaning of the breath holds the key to the vast treasury of divine explanations.

Our body functions without our conscious participation. The body is like a machine that runs according to the way it was designed. The Architect of this machine is the One who completely understands how it works. Why? Because this Architect is the One who not only designed it, but also created it. Couldn't this Architect then be considered to be "great?" Would you not want to know this Architect? Would you not want to be as close as you could be to this Brilliant Master?

Let's think about this a little. If we could understand the pure explanations to our fundamental questions, wouldn't this knowledge bring tremendous peace to the inner heart? There is an explanation, and it exists within our very own breath. Secrets lie within the conscious breath. So, how might we understand these secrets through our breath? Air delivers oxygen to our body and to the cells within our blood, without which, we would die. Yet, there is another body within our body that lies within the formlessness of our inner heart. This is our soul, our true self, which is one with the Pure Light of our Creator. How can we give life to that inner body of the soul? We must give it the oxygen of wisdom that intermingles with the intention to know God. We must have that intention firmly planted within our heart. Then we must learn how to breathe that formless breath of gratitude.

If the breath is the gift to life, shouldn't we be grateful for this gift? In this world, we take and take and take; yet we have no gratitude. Our life has been given to us for a reason; it is not a random act to be overlooked. We require determination to find the truth, to find the explanations of life. If we do not look for these understandings, how are we supposed to find them? Once we acquire faith, determination, surrender and gratitude, we will be able to pursue and achieve our goals.

God is the Most Compassionate Father. He gives endlessly to all for His children's sakes. God wants us to join with Him by understanding who we truly are. He is a Father who wants us to find Him by finding our true inner heart. Why would God create us and then just leave us? We separate ourselves from God through our doubts, ignorance and lack of faith. This state of darkness is created by our own mind. God will never leave us. Once we understand this, we can proceed and understand the purpose of our life, the truth of life, and our story.

# STEP 6

# Breathe

---

## Meditate with every breath

*(Note to reader: This section is best read when sitting down in a quiet place.)*

Think of gratitude. Think of being bestowed the greatest gift. Then think of the feeling of love towards the Giver of these gifts. Let that feeling fill your inner heart. Let your inner heart melt in the warmth of that love. Merge with that love. Feel the love. Be the receiver and the giver. Feel the gratitude.

*(Note to reader: Take your time when reading this.)*

Be awake and focus on your breath going in and out. Feel the harmony of it. Just look at it for a while.

As you exhale, allow all of the ignorance, sadness, pain, heaviness, and worry that are within you to leave. Slowly let your love for God merge with the inhaling of your breath. Feel the praise for God, feel His love enter you. Exhale all that is negative. Let it all go. Inhale with gratitude for God, praising Him with your humble breath. Exhale all that is negative. Let it all go. Feel the peace.

As you keep doing this, little by little your inner heart will become restored and alive. This internal cleansing of the body, mind, and heart will heal you and make you happy. This is a happiness not based in this world. It is based within your inner heart, attained purely by your own efforts.

This is how we liberate ourselves from suffering. Once we open our eye of wisdom to look beyond the veils of the physical world, the path of insight and clarity will open before us.

# Last Word

This is my journey and my guide. All that I have learned from my teacher M.R. Bawa Muhaiyaddeen (May God be pleased with him), along with my personal experiences, I am sharing with you. It is through suffering with my own illness that the intention to write this book came to be. It is my sincere prayer that the extraordinary powers of faith be revealed to all those who seek it. May all who suffer from the illnesses of this world discover that true lasting comfort and peace exists within their own hearts.

May God bless and help each person who reads this guidebook. God is the only Guide. May He Guide all who seeks His Truth. I ask for forgiveness for anything in this book that may have caused offense. I am merely sharing the tools of faith that I have found to be essential on my journey.

If we can generate belief in that One Power of Love and remain open, every day is an opportunity to learn and grow.

Love, to all.

# About the Author

**Julie R. Schelling** is a certified life coach. She received her coaching certifications from the Teleos Leadership Institute and the International Coach Federation. She is a graduate of the Mindfulness-Based Stress Management Program at the University of Pennsylvania and practices mindfulness meditation on a daily basis and incorporates mindfulness into her coaching practice. Julie supports her clients in their self-development and in the discovery process of finding their lives' noble purpose. She is a lifelong student of the Sufi teachings of M. R. Bawa Muhaiyaddeen. Julie currently resides outside of Philadelphia, PA.

Made in the USA
Charleston, SC
29 August 2014